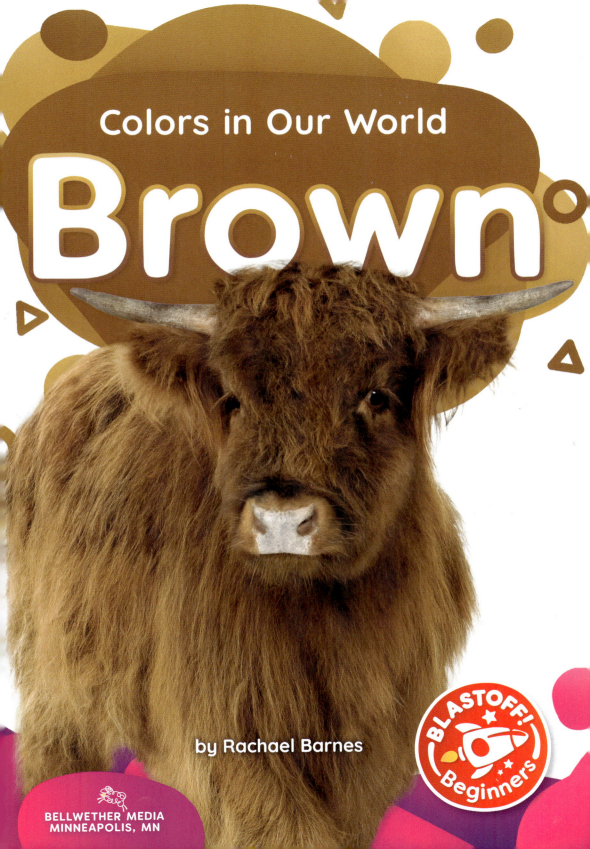

Colors in Our World

Brown

by Rachael Barnes

BLASTOFF! Beginners

BELLWETHER MEDIA
MINNEAPOLIS, MN

Blastoff! Beginners are developed by literacy experts and educators to meet the needs of early readers. These engaging informational texts support young children as they begin reading about their world. Through simple language and high frequency words paired with crisp, colorful photos, Blastoff! Beginners launch young readers into the universe of independent reading.

Sight Words in This Book

a	has	it	them	water
and	have	make	these	where
are	help	many	they	you
brown	in	see	this	
do	is	some	too	

This edition first published in 2026 by Bellwether Media, Inc.

No part of this publication may be reproduced in whole or in part without written permission of the publisher. For information regarding permission, write to Bellwether Media, Inc., Attention: Permissions Department, 3500 American Blvd W, Suite 150, Bloomington, MN 55431.

Library of Congress Cataloging-in-Publication Data

LC record for Brown available at: https://lccn.loc.gov/2025001568

Text copyright © 2026 by Bellwether Media, Inc. BLASTOFF! BEGINNERS and associated logos are trademarks and/or registered trademarks of Bellwether Media, Inc. Bellwether Media is a division of FlutterBee Education Group.

Editor: Betsy Rathburn   Designer: Laura Sowers

Printed in the United States of America, North Mankato, MN.

Table of Contents

Brown in the Forest	4
Brown Is All Around!	6
A Helpful Color	14
Brown Facts	22
Glossary	23
To Learn More	24
Index	24

Brown in the Forest

These brown bears climb a tree. They hold onto tree **bark**!

bark

Brown Is All Around!

Many animals are brown. Some plants are, too!

This monkey has brown fur. Many birds have brown **feathers**.

feathers

Some snakes and fish are brown. They have brown **scales**.

scales

Some plants grow brown nuts. Some plants make brown **spices**!

spices

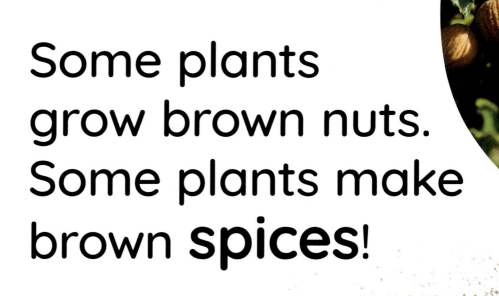

A Helpful Color

Brown fur helps animals hide. Brown feathers do, too.

Plants need sun and water. Leaves turn brown without them.

Brown dirt
is in gardens.
It helps
plants grow!

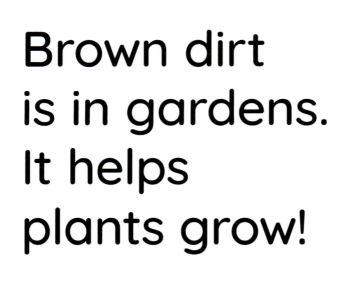

Where do you see brown in nature?

20

Brown Facts

Brown in Nature

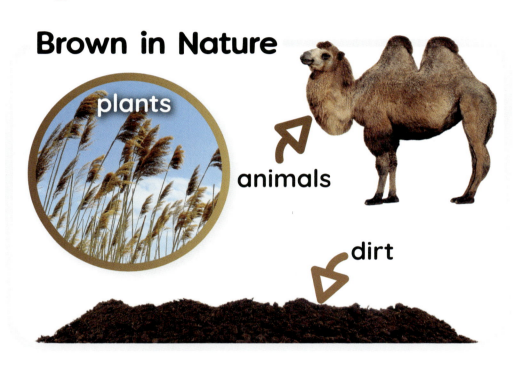

plants

animals

dirt

Why Is Nature Brown?

help animals hide

show need for sun and water

help plants grow

Glossary

bark

the tough outer layer of some plants

feathers

the outer coverings of birds

scales

small, hard plates that cover an animal's body

spices

parts of plants used to add flavor to food

To Learn More

ON THE WEB

FACTSURFER

Factsurfer.com gives you a safe, fun way to find more information.

1. Go to www.factsurfer.com.

2. Enter "brown" into the search box and click 🔍.

3. Select your book cover to see a list of related content.

Index

animals, 6, 14
bark, 4
birds, 8
brown bears, 4
dirt, 18, 19
feathers, 8, 14
fish, 10
fur, 8, 9, 14
gardens, 18
hide, 14
leaves, 16, 17
monkey, 8
nature, 20
nuts, 12, 13
plants, 6, 12, 16, 18
scales, 10
snakes, 10
spices, 12
tree, 4

The images in this book are reproduced through the courtesy of: Eric Isselee, front cover, p. 10; zevana, p. 3; Kuzmenko Viktoria photografer, p. 4; Erik Mandre, pp. 4-5; Abramova Kseniya, p. 6; LFRabanedo, pp. 6-7; iqbaldesigner, p. 8; Carlovis, pp. 8-9; Rich Carey, pp. 10-11; xpixel, pp. 12-13 (spices); Ansarphotographer, pp. 12-13; Harry Collins Photography, pp. 14-15; Sarah2, p. 16; FotoDuets, pp. 16-17; maxbelchenko, pp. 18-19; Tsekhmister, p. 20; tanit123, pp. 20-21; AlinaMD, p. 22 (plants); photomaster, p. 22 (animals); Food Impressions, p. 22 (dirt); Sapodorado26, p. 22 (help animals hide); smthtp, p. 22 (show need for sun and water); malshkoff, p. 22 (help plants grow); Parinussa Revy, p. 23 (bark); matushaban, p. 23 (feathers); Ken Griffiths, p. 23 (scales); Symonenko Viktoriia, p. 23 (spices).